The Story Thus...

Eclipse Side B

Eclipse, Volume 2

Sakari Lacross

Published by Sakari Lacross, 2024.

ECLIPSE SIDE B

First edition. August 4, 2024.

ISBN: 979-8230891567

Written by Sakari Lacross.

Table of Contents

Everything Untold

If you were mine...

I'd press the idea of two more

A boy and a girl

With your name and mine

It'll be after some time

If you were mine...

There's a sea of subtitles I'd drag us to

We'd be more than a long-term thing

Like the sun and the sky

Everything would be guaranteed

~ Sakari

Let me drown in your waist

Unbelievable waters, against my chin

Legs ever so laxed over my shoulders

Lying down on your back, you can't be thinking of him

~ Sakari

The last time you needed me

My jeans stayed on

That's all we had time for

I couldn't get you undressed

I couldn't see you in your purest

~ Sakari

The way you feel, you have to go first

The feeling of you, is such an inspiration

Wrapped around me, so enduring

It'll be an endless wish, if you could go twice before me

~ Sakari

He doesn't define you.

Hide away from his insecurities

And I'll be the one to find you

I don't mind

The back and forth texts

You can stay over

Until you believe him again.

~ Sakari

And so you're beautiful for yourself

I'll always believe you

Likes all over your page

All of those people act like they need you

~ Sakari

From Cover To Cover

Those convulsions in your waist

You hold my head against

And I'm doing my best

To catch all of your wet wishes

~ Sakari

I understand you, like our last kiss

That wasn't supposed to happen, but it did

So whenever you feel like it, you can come back over

Whenever you feel like it, you can come back

~ Sakari

Honestly, does he deserve you back?

You're so much better to him, than he is to you

Is he purposely hurting you?

It feels like it, doesn't it?

~ Sakari

It was always with pleasure

That I held your legs up

Moments now different for you

In favor of you

~ Sakari

That last exhale you pushed

Right as I made my way through

I wanted to hold that clip of you

In my head forever

~ Sakari

I'm not overthinking

Slow sips of you, I anticipate

Starting from your chest

My head starts to gravitate

~ Sakari

Missing Pages

I'm liking you so much

Can we have sex this time

On my back I'll go

You can take the lead this time

~ Sakari

I'm doing much better

When I've just slid right out of you

I'm not as confused or hurt

When you convince me of my insecurities, in this way

It's all in my head

When you're reminding me in this way

~ Sakari

And it was never about looks to you

He just takes up so much of your time

And he's supposed to do that, right?

You're committed to him...

~ Sakari

When you pretend that I'm there

What are we actually doing

Are you prepping a meal for two

Knowing that there will be leftovers

***

What are we actually doing?

***

Do we take action in the kitchen

You leaned over the counter

Do we get the chance to close the curtains

Knowing that he's friends with your neighbors

***

What are we actually doing?

***

~ Sakari

On top of everything, on top of you

On top of the kitchen table, on top of you

On top of your staircase, I get on top of you

On the topic at hand, I'm always trying to stay, on top of you

~ Sakari

I wanna gather all my friends, and tell them about you

But I know they'll want to meet you, so what do I say

This standstill feels like a line, the longest yet

I'm out of line, but I'm not leaving yet

~ Sakari

Chills Around My Heart

You're on my heart, for right now

Chest pains, I already know how

Continuous mood swings, but I calm down

You put your lips on me; I calm down

This will end, once it ends

You're someone I desire, for right now

~ Sakari

I'm in her flowers, a field so deep

Cherished and fathomable

In her bed, I can't sleep

So we'd never sleep

I'd never let you drift

In my arms, you'll remain restless

Assignments of offers

Check them off for me

~ Sakari

I bet we'd mark her bed

I bet her and I will pull and plant more of her flowers

Like picturing my teeth against her neck

Doesn't she sound so tasteful

Exotic? I never had

Like stains in her bed...

Stains in her bed...

~ Stains In Her Bed

Your Comfort Zone

I'm blushing as I go

Lower than your stomach

Seeing and feeling

How smooth everything is

~ Sakari

After everything, I'm holding you

Like we're repeatedly having sex together, for the first time

I'm holding you

It's simple, when I'm in love with you

~ Sakari

I'm holding your heart with care

I know it's been dropped so many times

The same way I'll be holding you

Is how I value your trauma

~ Sakari

Sometimes I go silent

Just know that I'm thinking

About what else to give you

To show you I love you

~ Sakari

Yes I can fall in love

With my bestfriend

You're the best

At accepting me

~ Sakari

Lying in your bed together

And we're watching tv

Though you always go to sleep

And I'm always giving you late

Goodnight kisses

~Sakari

Hopefully The Story Doesn't End...

Angel Lips

There's a sunrise in our background

Your bed is so close to the window

All night we've been in love

~ Sakari

Life begins to sound like static

When your arms are around my neck

And I'm presenting myself, on top of you

~ Sakari

This year has to be something great

We came into it

On a Thursday night

~ Sakari

Pull me back into your paradise

Every time work calls

~ Sakari

In every fantasy, I'm yours

Along every river, you belong to me

~ Sakari

I live in a fantasy

You'll be mine

In every world I create

~ Sakari

Little Light

I want to consume you entirely

Your bed can be the platter

Pieces of you, all over

~ Sakari

Hearts For Lease

You think about it.

Every time he fucks up

You think about it.

All it takes is a text

And I'll meet you wherever.

Remember, you can go back to him

No hard feelings to tell

I know all of you doesn't exist

I can make due, with only a piece

~ Sakari

I give myself away to them

To those that reach

But nothing feels real

Nothing to believe

~ Sakari

There's no embarrassment to it

I'm trying hard not to go numb

My choice of drug is sex

Lie down with me please

~ Sakari

I'm just ready to be true

To stop meeting you, only in the shower

To ask you out for once

Instead of asking you, to get on top

~ Sakari

The last time I cried, I was inside of you

The feeling of you, brought tears to my eyes

~ Sakari

Nephilim

You've been so pretty, I must confess

Pin my wrist down, and jump on top

Nine times in a row, nine nights in a row

~ Sakari

Know that I manifested your liquids, pouring down

And I would be underneath you

Feeling mixtures of warmth and heat

~ Sakari

Why do you feel so tense

This feels like a clear distraction

What am I taking you away from

~ Sakari

There was you, my only sound of music

You were on beat with our body drums

You were our lead vocalist

~ Sakari

You appear to be free, but you're shackled inside

So sex has become your release

I've got the key, inside

~ Sakari

We can't be honest with each other

We're both touching another

No need for confessions now

~ Sakari

Lie down and get lost with me

Turn on your side and become found

Arch on all four, and be mine

~ Sakari

Don't miss out!

Visit the website below and you can sign up to receive emails whenever Sakari Lacross publishes a new book. There's no charge and no obligation.

https://books2read.com/r/B-A-GXQL-CLICE

BOOKS 2 READ

Connecting independent readers to independent writers.

Did you love *Eclipse Side B*? Then you should read *Flames Unversed*[1] by Sakari Lacross!

[2]

Something calls them. A beacon of absolute power. This same beacon summons something else. A deity for those it has called, to face. Kayden, a sorcerer of fire, faces this deity. However, with his flames not truly being tamed, he struggles to even match the deity's power.

---

1. https://books2read.com/u/471Noa

2. https://books2read.com/u/471Noa

Also by Sakari Lacross

A Dawn Breaking Romance

Romance Dawn

Beyond Dawn

A Final World

Rising Tides

Don't End Up Consumed

Don't End Up Consumed 2

Belonging

I Hope I Belong

I Hope I Belong Too

Eclipse

Eclipse: Side A

Eclipse Side B

Perfect Gentleman

Perfect Gentleman

Simp Undying

I Simp For You

I Simp For You Too

Another Reason To Simp

Soft Hardcover

New Love Plus(+)

Sunset Szn

Sunset Szn

Sunset SZN 2

Sunset SZN 3

The Last Witch

The Last Witch: Book 1

The Last Witch: Book 2

This Is For Her

Someone Like You

Someone Like You Too

Someone Else Like You

Threads

Threads

Standalone

The Legend Of Krampus

Deeper Than Magic

A Place Inside My Castle

Luminary

Loyalist To The Moon

Thoughts & Memories

Ideas & Reality

Vines & Beauty

V For Her

Playing With Skeletons

About the Author

Sakari Lacross was born February 5th, 1994, in Cleveland Ohio. Spending most of his childhood being raised in Flint Michigan, Sakari's mother moved him and his family to Arizona when he was 15. Sakari has been writing since he was nine years old, competing in his school's poetry contest and bimonthly writing events. Discovering all his true potential to write during his years he went to linden charter academy, Sakari won his first local poetry contest at Sam Garcia Western Avenue Library, located in Avondale Arizona. Sakari then published his first poetry collection, titled, PTSD.

www.ingramcontent.com/pod-product-compliance
Lightning Source LLC
LaVergne TN
LVHW091228150826
845673LV00003B/1057

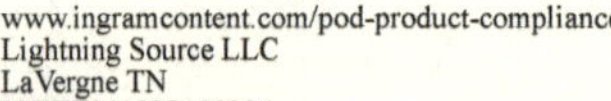

* 9 7 9 8 2 3 0 8 9 1 5 6 7 *